Diaspora Blues

Ali Jimale Ahmed

THE RED SEA PRESS

Trenton | London | New Delhi | Cape Town | Nairobi | Addis Ababa | Asmara | Ibadan

THE RED SEA PRESS
541 West Ingham Avenue | Suite B
Trenton, New Jersey 08638

Cover and book design: Roger Dormann

Library of Congress Cataloging-in-Publication Data

Ahmed, Ali Jimale.
 Diaspora blues / Ali Jimale Ahmed.
   p. cm.
 ISBN 1-56902-238-0 (cloth) -- ISBN 1-56902-239-9 (pbk.)
 1. Somalia--Poetry. 2. Somalis--Foreign countries--Poetry. I. Title.
 PR9396.9.A37D53 2005
 821'.914--dc22
                         2005003631

To
All people who are
Languishing, flourishing, frolicking
Grieving, grinning, groaning
In voluntary or forced exile

And to all the
Internally Displaced Persons
Of an Africa that's still in the grip
Of an ever widening yet transient
Doldrums.

Contents

I. Whither History?
Francis Fukayama's Whoopla

II. Spear Dance

III. America, Our America

IV. Of Meditations Murky and Muddled

V. Where to, Africa?

VI. The Aloe Taste of Exile

I

Whither History?
Francis Fukayama's Whoopla

What brings a house down?
Is it the keening of insects, the snails
Blithering up deaf walls?
—Paula Closson Buck, "The Acquiescent Villa"

MacArthur Park and Tiananmen Square

I don't care whether the cat is black or
White, so long as it can catch the mouse.
—Deng Xiaoping

Mounted police in full swing
Neighing horses not seen since
My boyhood days around Stadio Conis
On the edge of ravaging sand dunes across
Lazaretto asylum where those wheezing
Of consumption and those plagued by Frenzy's
Fury flirted with one another and in full
View of the only chaperone on duty
Herself afflicted with laughing sickness

Those erstwhile memories gain perspicacity
In the slow motion of mounted police
In pursuit of a fringe group of radicals
Fixated on celebrating the First of May
In the center of MacArthur Park
In Los Angeles.

The media report a scuffle
Between police and protestors
Without bothering to explain
What the scuffle was all about.

That long-forgotten image
Molasses of molten larva forged in
The smithy of one's first impressions of being in
Liberty's sacrosanct abode came crawling
Creeping in my head last night
Last night as thousands under cover of
Darkness converged on Tiananmen Square
In Beijing.

5

Like zealots of literacy campaigns
Ready to catapult a nation into
The throes of a new age, or install
A new mind equipped to sneak
Out of the shadow of the old leopard
Now lost in history's cruel sinuosity
The old leopard who eons ago divined
The long walk out of what he deemed
A dead-end to nowhere for a nation
Destined to hatch a second time.

Last night all routes leading to Tiananmen
Court were sealed off as were those leading to
The Park 15 years ago. A magnet court
A magnet park potential breeding soil for all
Agents provocateurs paid hoodlums traitors prodded on
From afar and across oceans
Famed open spaces are
The parchments where the new lesson of a victor
First savors the light of day. A victor because
An adversary is always run out of town.

At the Park
The protestors mime the words
Of a leader long driven into exile
Yet the words take a life of their own
Defining the landscape in terms of days past
The police also follow a script
Calligraphed before by a neurotic
Long gone with his visions of demons gnawing,
Gnawing at the fabric of freedom's house
Visions, you would think, fit for asylum
Were it not for the fact the schizophrenic
Was the chief warden of the cuckoo's nest
And the one entrusted to judge
Whether the emperor had any clothes

So the era of a temporary suspension of sanity
Itself symptomatic of earlier sisterly moments
Ushers in the epoch of the Contagion:
Demonic spread of infectious silence of eerie proportions
And the creepy convictions of the silent that
The victims had it coming lubricates
The shaming ritual of nincompoops caught in
A whirlwind of obscene dances unbecoming American

And the circus stops at several zoos
Where a zoo manager or the one harboring umbrage
Sacrifices someone at the altar of self-preservation
Many who thought they had procured
Immunity to the disease of the nincompoops
Now witness their immunity being withdrawn
On the uncorroborated account of a jilted lover
Or the notarized testimony of an ambitious co-worker
Or simply, just simply, the ranting of a wretched soul
Scared out of its wits

So it went, so it went till the fetid
Stench of carcasses pervaded everywhere and
The arrow still up in the air the silent multitude
Disciples of Pan sighed with exhausted fear,
"This is not what it was supposed to be."
As though witch-hunts ever envisage
The scope of their writ. Let the chips
Fall where they may rarely includes
The mouth that utters the edict
And the chips fall anywhere but

At the Gate of Heavenly Peace
Deathwatch attendants by the bedside of the old dung
Scramble to stem a tide unleashed by
The old beetle's memorable maxim about cats and mice
A slip of the tongue that sent him to
A boot camp.
The throng at the Court chant
Of the inefficacy of the cats now in vogue

Ali Jimale Ahmed

SOS

Concerned with the fate of the cats now in vogue
A trickster friend sent this prescription:

Rhubarb rhizome in the raw
To supplement
A Purina deli-cat(e) diet to help
Energize the faltering strides of
Cats unfamiliar with gourmet treats
And in a renewed élan redouble
The efforts of the late beetle now
Mummified in Mao silk suits
To inspire surviving hands to roll
Mounds of human dung off
Hallowed grounds reserved for
Flexible feet of unbound ambition.

The Tovarishes and the Scrolls[1]

> *Next morning he was seen at the station*
> *buying a ticket for Kurovskoye,*
> *a village much like ours, only smaller.*
> —Louis Simpson, "Caviare at the Funeral"

At the crossroads, the tovarishes hesitated
A wrong turn would mean death. Yet
All the turns looked eerily the same
A tovarish that left no other bequest suggested
They flip a coin. But others doubted
If such a decision would be wise
To divine the future with the flip of a coin
To decide with a toss when life and
More than life was at stake

Beyond that the scrolls are silent
Rendering it impossible to decipher
What really transpired at the gathering
Of the tovarishes at the crossroads.

The distant image of an imago sweltering
On the margins of Serendip now taunts
The sensibilities of a group yet unsired

A future historian rummages through the scrolls
Peruses bears the pain of waiting as
Years of fertile persistence yield the shadow
Linings of six stubborn words hanging loose

---

[1] The six Russian words in the poem mean, respectively: parliament, a beverage of fermented cow's milk, bread, consciousness, truth, and time.

9

The argus-eyed unravels the Cyrillic
Riddle wrapped inside an enigma
(Sir Winston, where are you now?
Sir Winston, could you proffer a thought?)
The argus-eyed dances with delectations
As *duma, kefir, kheleb, soznanie*
Pravda, and *vremya* dance off the scrolls

A seventh word, not in Cyrillic, casts
Doubt on the historian's early inclinations
The word in Roman alphabet is either
Comparison or caparison prompting the historian to
Annotate a whole section with an obelus.

Beyond that the historian is nowhere near a reading

In exasperation, he throws his hands up in the air. Sighs.
"Was it a premeditated murder or just
A mishap bound to happen?"

The forensic evidence suggests sudden
Death on impact, preceded by a slow
Death crafted onto the body of the first tovarishes
In the trenches of the First March.

A signature lurking at the bottom of
A badly mauled scroll sports
A morsel of a name in Morse code—

- .. -.- .. ... .- .. .-..

Isla Negra

I leave my house by the Seaside
in Isla Negra to the labor unions
—Pablo Neruda, "Testament"

The conch in the dream
A dream in a conch
Footprints of a snail
Sinuous slow suggestive
Past present future
The robber of footprints dastardly delusive
Fries in bonfires
Concealed behind spider
Webs of labyrinthine architecture
Carved to lure hasty travelers
Chaperoned from afar

After the event
The old wizard of words
Counts the spleen of flayed mules
Showcased at the bull pen of hell
Heap upon heap
Endowed with lucid tongues
Relay the tale how
Ricocheted bullets
Augustan awesome
Escorted some to early sleep

Years later, much later
The old wizard of words
Doesn't wake to non-being
As the other side of the page now
Rejoices in the turning of tables
The drip drop of the innocent

Fancy their vindications
As curdles of clots
Lead espying eyes
Back to retreating footprints
Left behind by encapuchados
Hooded hoodlums
Unmasked by the slow gait of time
Moving at a snail's pace.

Metempsychosis

Skewed out of shape the nation
As an echo of your identity
Tilts southward
Sublimating the earth
With insipid supplications
Insidious lamentations that mourn
The loss of the only dromedary
In the communal corral

The camel's initial gallant gait
Has long since given way to a
Galumph forcing the rustler to
Confront a hideous metempsychosis
The erstwhile dead have now hoisted
A house in his body.

Ali Jimale Ahmed

Homage

Seventy years of lived life
Served on the pinhead of a sled
And adorned in innocence
Leap scorpions to awful yearnings
That sidle sideways before
They slink away into the woods.

The sled commemorates a life slouching
Sideways paying homage to the base
Of humble beginnings.

II

All endings, including this one
Point to and from
Small beginnings. Only this time
The sled endures a second caress
By the feeble hand of a destiny
Dethroned twice.

(Pause)

Gravy

A stolen she-camel, so goes the saying,
Never begets a *halal* calf, yet
Robber barons slough off
Vestiges of their old wicked ways
To beget kosher enterprises at least
Viewed as such by those nourished
By leftover gravy scraped off
The bottom of a swindler's cauldron
Apologetic (retroactive?) appraisal of
The swindler's blemishes inaugurates
A palinode of myriad perplexity:
The past's unsavory gait
Begot us and much depends on
What was done with the stolen she-camel.

II

Spear Dance

If I sound defensive it's because I'm tired sometimes. I saw
a calf born without skin.
—Kimiko Hahn, "The Calf" in *Earshot*

Ali Jimale Ahmed

Operation Elephantine

He [Saddam Hussein] came from a brittle land,
a frontier country between Persia and Arabia, with little
claim to culture and books and grand ideas.
—Fouad Ajami

And the apache helicopters
Deadly with a long range fart
Shower on the enemy skunk-like emissions
Swirling over the skies of Old Mesopotamia,
The Fertile Crescent referred to,
By he who should know better,
By Ajami whose name reflects
Paradoxical pointers to self and other,
As a barren cesspit that never produced
Knowledge fit for human consumption
Clear testimony that
Ignorance is not always the result
Of not being privy to the facts.

The Thief of Oxen

To blur reality
Is what Blair did
In the interest of plurality
Of forging a common stand against
Tyranny, the mother of all blurriness.

Blurring
In the interest of Blair
Would be a crime, but
In the interest of truth resembles
The thief of oxen in the myth
Who herded the bull by the tail.
Dragging a swish backwards
Is best left for understanding
A life that's already lived.

Cannibalism

"This cannibalism must stop!"
Roared the cowboy at the helm of the House
Before he was made homeless
His heir apparent danced
On the floor full of regal colors

The teacher of history forgot a
Key lesson in his profession:
History mimics its old shadow too often
To hoist us by our own petard

And when the time came the Professor, too,
Had to go the same way as the Texan
His words succinct
And with no tincture of dubiety echoed
The Texan's farewell musings without
The twang: "This cannibalism must end."

Punished by Cleo, the Professor of
History wallows in dirt,
Which now out of its place,
Besmears the sensibility of others.

Psychotic Cops

At the recruiting booth
A mean-looking wannabe
Cop looks intently into
The eyes of the recruiting officer
"And why do you want to become a policeman?"
I heard on the news that a cop
Killer is on the loose
"So?"
So, I want to kick his arse and then, you know
Apprehend him and things like that
"I'm not sure if you are interviewing for the right job.
This is the police booth, you know, not
Killers for hire."

No, sir, believe me, you need headhunters
Someone with my credentials
Sharp reflexes forged in
The smithy of Dukeian furnaces
I'm an ever-ready hand undoubting of our mission
To spray DDT
To weed out the burden in our midst
You see, sir, the tattoo on my
Right arm—the emblem of the
Undoubting Tom who shoots first and
Asks questions later. You remember, sir,
The Mandingo killed near the zoo,
It's a jungle out there
The noise the chirping sound the roar that
Intoxicates you with fear hate more fear
Always jittery always on the lookout for a
Stray cobra or a tiger on the loose
It's at that moment one really feels

The crushing chill in the bone that
Kurtz must have felt in

The bosom of darkness
You follow my drift, sir
You feel it
It's no longer a yarn spun
Out of someone else's experience
This is history, sir, and I
Am ready to do battle with the devil
In the jungle near the zoo.
And until we divine a zoo for the one
That looks—*no, he is not inhuman*—
But reminds us of our connection to the
Now-gone prehensile part of our rump
Until then I assure you, sir,
We need to be vigilant
Have our night vision goggles on and
Have a gun in hand ready and
If need be a bazooka
Or even a plunge

The interviewing officer murmurs stammers
"Could you excuse me for a minute
let me consult with my boss
I'll be right back!"

Vision on Hind Legs[2]

I had a series of unsettling dreams last night
Yevtushenko was talking about Che
Walcott was reminiscing an earlier lament
On poetic renditions of mishaps on the heels
Of a death foretold

Last night I had a series of unsettling dreams
In a nightmarish stupor I saw
Lorca's grave on the left side of
A mountain slope on the shores of
An Andalus in the grip of Aznar
The mini moo of a troika
Now in desperate haste to catch
A time machine back to 1096.

I had a vision last night
Of minute men in post
Apocalyptic uniforms hurling
MOABs at Orpah's offspring
Mother of all bombs meant to
Deter the confrontational captain of
Orpah's team in desperate haste to catch
A glimpse of the Old Tower of yonder.

[2] The biblical Orpah is the sister of Ruth, who, with their mother-in-law Naomi, wanted to go to Bethlehem. Only at the last minute, does Orpah decide to stay in Moab. Coined by Defense Department officials, the acronym "MOAB" refers to "mother of all bombs."

First Cousins

The Arab is a Semite
Begotten on the run
In the wilderness

The Jew is the Semite
Sired during the halcyon days of
A Patriarch now wrapped in the hands of
A second wife blessed to be
An Eve in the incarnate

Later ages are urged to
Be matrilineal as a surety against
The Arab now the other Semite
Alterity graced with a definite article

The Arab is anti-Semite
His suavity lost in the wilderness

The Arab and the Jew
The Jew and the Arab
First cousins caught in a
Whirlpool of totemic dance
Designed from without to
Mesmerize mock-heroic combatants
Unable to jump in the fray
Until the Second Coming.

(*Pause*)

Poetry is like a swoon, with this difference:
it brings you to your senses.
—Charles Bernstein, "The Klupzy Girl"

Ali Jimale Ahmed

The Globe

Falling objects go down, go south
Flying objects go up, go north
And that is how my contest
With the globe came into being
I stared at it, it stared back at me
Our stares unblinking coterminous pernicious
A contest of wills ensued

Then slowly in my stare
The globe tripped over
Turned upside down
The north falling, falling down
Going south, the south ascending
Going north, soaring toward the sky

And then … and then …
A poetic swoon overwhelmed my stare
My stare has only reclaimed
A way of looking at things
As old and creepy
As the object in its gaze.

III

America, Our America

Bees

La nina, il nino
Africanized bees
Revenants of erstwhile
Subdued spirits
Now reincarnated in
Bee bodies

Russian cold
West Nile virus
Canadian flu
Japanese sneeze
Mexican insects
Asian beetle and other
Assorted hordes accustomed to
Sneaking in without passports

All intent on licking
Dry the honey and milk
Harnessed over the ages

The only plague the blessed ever produced
Is a prankster appropriately named
Dennis the Menace
Nee Timothy McVeigh
The homegrown derelict
who almost evaded
Scrutiny reserved for
Mr. Death Wish with accent.

Camel Meat at JFK

At Osaka International Airport, the Immigration
Officer scrutinizes my travel document
"American?"
No.
"Where are you from?"
Somalia. But I now
Am a person without a state
Coming from the states.

Looks at my letter of invitation
"O, Osaka Institute of Technology
You are a scientist?"

Afraid to dampen his enthusiasm now that
The pendulum is in my favor
I advise my mouth to circumvent the query

Circumspection is the hallmark
Of a soul short on somersaults
Not really, I mumble the words

Across the hall the familiar face of
My host beams through the crowd
Then—a bombshell easily detonated

"You have cocaine?"
What?
"Drugs?"

Perturbed by the fool's question
I stammer through the snafu
No, no drugs.

And the stamp of approval precedes
Its twin sister—"Welcome."

Fifteen days later, at JFK
The same ritual is repeated
Only this time, the subtlety
The veneer of courtesy shown at Osaka Airport
Succumbs to naked stupidity

"Where you on this flight?"

No. I descended on from on high the ceiling
Now, what kind of question is that?
Do I look like a stowaway?

Yes, sir, I came with these people
Pointing to Japanese fellow passengers
It's early in the morning
We seem to be early birds.

The next flight out of JFK was more bizarre
"Sir," the young African American lady at the scanner
Machine intones, "There are
Traces of explosives on your carry-on."
Explosives? You're kidding?
"No."
And in a tone that reveals the seriousness
Of the matter, she asks me to unlock
The bosom of my bag. Nothing there.

How would I tell her that
I have no death wish.
In a sarcastic tone mostly meant to lash back at
Stupidity perpetrated on behalf of a puppeteer
By one of your kind I hammer at her
Raw fetid fuzzy
Oh, I forgot …

"What did you forget?"
You know, my cousin who fights for
Hizballah in the Shouf Mountains of Lebanon
Borrowed this very carry-on not long ago
So, this carry-on muled ammunition for Hizballah

"Really? Where is he now?"

The earnestness in her voice helped me to
Snap out of my crazed reverie as
I renege on a promise, it seems
I have already whispered into her ear

(How could I accuse her of using me to
get a medal befitting a patriot.)

Disavowing is the next best thing to
Wiggle out of the lizard's hole
I was just kidding ma'am
Am no relation to anyone fighting
For Hizballah.

Incredulity mixes with disappointment
Her voice no longer radiant trails
Tattered, she goes for the juggernaut
"You mean," she pauses
Spitting fiery syllables
"You have no relative fighting for
The Party of Allah?"

Unable to decipher whether
The question is as innocent as it sounds
Or a taunt to prod me into
A dejected brawlish bravado
I hide behind incantations
Don't give them a reason to maul you

Ali Jimale Ahmed

Bull dogs could kill with impunity when
Shielded by the puppeteer behind the closed
Door where she and I are intimately monitored
Don't fall into a familiar trap
Trap trap trap

I don't know myself
And if I did
Goethe be my witness
I would probably run away.

Subliminal

Of the beautiful body
Next to the sexy Chevrolet
The message is less subtle
To get the body, you need the car
Nothing new as all ads play on our
Insecurities and the masks needed to deflate
But the body next to a purchasable
Item itemizes the woman, already paid
To coo ogling eyes.

Jerks

On the F train to Manhattan
I couldn't help but overhear a
Conversation between two women
Rather a monologue or a sermon
As the one sitting to my immediate right
Is all but a vessel of ears

The braided one explains,
"Nothing good ever issued from their
loins. Even my allergies
have their genesis in their
indiscriminate jerking off sprinkling
dust-like semen that cause pain.
Talk about jerks with
no regard for others!"

Nirvana

And what did those drumbeats in the dark of the night
really mean? What did they portend?
—Ngugi, *Penpoints, Gunpoints, and Dreams*

And the good professor proclaims
Marilyn Monroe to be on par with
The Holy Book and the residue from
Waaq's era: an ostrich egg[3]

The driver on loan explains that
The three sustain him like
Jerky or kola nuts
On long nights on the road

The Professor speaking in a distinctly
American idiom calls the three
Fetishes that help the driver
Sally forth on an empty stomach

Also in America, another professor
This time American-born falls
Short of his early provocative propensities
As he explains Marable's echoes of the X man

"What are the drums saying?"
The two professors have a knack for
Deciphering the hidden tunes in advance
Of an all-out tom tom dance that is sure to
Bless the world with its grace
A tom tom dance that heals

---

[3] *Waaq* is the Sky God, a pre-Islamic deity among the Cushitic peoples of Northeast Africa. *Waaq* is also an Arabic word that means "defender." As far as I can remember, the word is mentioned twice in the Qur'an. See Surah 13:34 and 37.

Mends broken souls before propelling
Them onto higher grounds where
Collective nirvana is a must for
All private communions with the naked self
What are the drums saying?
I hear someone ask

Ask the professors.

Enron, Inc.

And Ron's fortuitous legacy of winning
The race for the Gipper has now metamorphosed
Into hellish howls of minions dried clean
Of life's legacy by mini Gippers mimicking
The old master's putrid show of schadenfreude
Mini Gippers gone rowdy with
Human blood on their whiskers—
Cannibals of Enron, Inc.
And of fellow travelers-turned dupes.

Viva Miguel

At Ground Zero—the sacred spot where
The twin sisters came to embrace the
Fundaments of their beginnings Migeul
Flanked by well wishers views the
Carnage visited upon a place
Going about its business.

The morning after
Vituperative finger pointing soothes
Sobers the frayed tempers of a party unwonted to
Wade through gibberish spun out of use by
Spin gurus in cozy smoke-filled rooms

Cherche la buit! Quick, quick before the
Shame spreads gnaws at the seams of the
Body-politic. Quick, quick find
The culprit who handed sweet victory to the
Enemy whose agnates trail our moiety by
A large margin. So the etymology of a defeat
Undeserved must seek meaning in the wily ways
Of a spoiler too clever to let bygones be
The unmarked tomb of a defeat undeserved.

Innuendos loud and whispered hurl
Insults at the sore loser desperate to
Assume a mantle too big for a zookeeper

And Miguel—just being Miguel dines the
Morning after with the zookeeper to
Suture the deep wounds that dot the
Deck of the ship he is about to navigate

And Miguel—just being Miguel chitchats with
The sharp tongue twister that refused to

Leave the zookeeper in the lurch
And Miguel—just being Miguel is able to
Read fissures in the bosom of
A party unable to sniff the air

Miguel's ascendancy to the lofty seat of
A lofty city envied by all jettaturas
Here and there near and far
Miguel's hooray heralds the dew line that will
Dampen the wings of a party still enveloped
In the misty days of Tammany Hall.

Reality TV

And before spring gave way to autumn
We were basking in the sunshine of
Fake bouts and contrived conniptions

In autumn Jerry's fields withered with
The multiple hankering for everything robust
Raw real surreal
Reality TV born on the heels of old quaint
Arranged bouts acted out on stage by actors
Eking out a living from circumstantial shame
The new actors are just real
Semantics without guise

Now, brother Jerry is stunned at
The lack of ingenuity in building on his
Exquisite genius at hosting *avant la lettre*
America's first reality TV.

Pig Latin

Specialists abound in America
Aprenda en una semana
¡llame a hora!

In America we are blessed with specialists who
Tax their brains so that the rest of us
Scatterbrains find meaning in life's
Vicissitudes follies and foibles

"Help!" I hear a mother scream
"I'm scared of my twinkled teen daughter!"

Juanita—the monster child bereft of
Filial piety prophesied in The Song
Of the family in La Paz calls her mother
"A fat bitch."

And I saw no mouth shrink to a stump.

Who you gonna call?

"Maury works hard to teach these teens."
The tinge in the sidekick's voice has
A farcical tone but Maury is set upon mending
A tongue not beholden to any head
Juanita & Co. are given a tour
Of the coroner's autopsy room across the street
The teens are shaken by the ghastly ghostly sight
Of cadavers harvested a hue before harvest time.

Across the street where Maury performs miracles
Talented tongue twisters abound
Some in Pig Latin astonishingly commune with
Dalmatians lamenting the loss of a companion
Fuzzy puffy didn't eat for days

In an adjacent room sits dog's worst
Leach unable to see what's in store for him
Send sister Cleo to the rescue
Cleo to do a free tarot reading
The muse of yonder weaves a yarn or two
Implicating our past in
The dirt on our doorstep

Sister Cleo divines so that we may see
Brother Maury presents a poetic rendition
Of simian psychosis without
A prehensile tail.

Specialists abound in America

Aprenda en una semana
!llame a hora!

Instant Gratification
(To the red-haired kid I grew up with)
RIP

From age three
He was like a son to me
Brilliant humane humorous suave
I thought I had rubbed some of
My charm on his brittle soul ready to
Absorb some of the ways of the wily.
He never saw his father whose
Silhouette shape was sewn into
The lower hems of his mother
He grew up with me
I grew up with him and
He had grown on me.

"Jimale," he once said,
"if I win a gold medal at the Olympics,"
I don't remember for what sport
the kid was multitalented,
"If I win a gold medal, what will
they say? 'An amazing white kid
whose talent is rarely seen in the
race,' or, finding out about my mixed
heritage, 'What did you expect—
excelling in sport runs in their genes.'"

And he laughed. A chill ran down my spine
Here was a 13-year-old kid giving me the inside scoop
Of an America still bedeviled by color politics

I don't know how I answered
His question more like a remark than a
Question. He is dead now
Dead at the age of 18

Dead at the hands of a man coveting
His wife. Gone. Snuffed.
Nubbed in the bud
In the primrose of life
A single shot to the head
Life taken with a single shot to the
Head to grant some lout a rogue
Gratification that merges the trigger with
Fidgety fingers that cede
No ground to insane calls for
A desire retamed.

(Pause)

The Poet
(Of Ezra, the Pound)

And when the scribe
Who was worth his weight
In sterling sang
The praises of the Duce
The denizens of the world wondered
What signals he was gathering from
His wacky warped antennae.

IV

Of Meditations Murky and Muddled

When no smoke ascends
from the hamlets,
when you can't smell fire
from a distance
in the rain.

You know no tea is boiling
on the three stones of the campfire ...

—Abdirahman Mirreh, "When Nomads Move,"
in *From an Acacia Landscape*

Leaves

The nomadic streak in me
Reckons wisdom in leaves
Taking leave before the
Onslaught of wintry bites

Life is in trust with you
Run, run for your life

The good side of my soul
Contested as always and
In contestation with itself
Reckons foresight in leaves
Taking leave before frostbites

The strong shield the weak
By freeing them of filial duties
Sending the young to a hideaway
Where they remain unseen

Smothered by a wide white blanket
The cuckoo leaves
Imprints of a wider wily wisdom
Pretend to be hugging their mother
Till the next season

The other side of my soul
Frowns at the perennial ingenuity
Of making virtue of expediency
The leaves are the castaways jettisoned
Before the onslaught of the white marshal.

Post-Ism

House: Hyphen: Hybrid
In the tropic fields of our discourses
In the tropologic meanderings of our lives
In the mosaic fiefdoms of our Diasporas
In the glorious reign of "psychic distances"
A globetrotter hums a howl
Like a voice hollering its own humbug
Hampering historicity
Hiding its own hype.

Totem

Our national totem the chameleon
Has blessed us
With a foresight to calligraph
Time and Place
Being and Time
Tear and Laughter
Through the switch of a twinkle
With the twinkle of the eyelids.

Magic Potion

He concocted a potion
That killed a human being
He—the weaver of death
His white magic—the noose

She concocted a potion
That let the imagination set sail
She—the molder of life
Her black magic—the footprint
Left behind by the weave of
The rushes hastily making way for yet
Another pallet.

Shibboleth

A cordate leaf left at the scene
Lends lacerating memory to leap
Forth: a burlap sack, two pairs of rubber
Beach thongs unable to embrace
A prophecy mauled in deliverance.

Hawa/Eve

And all that is
Bad belongs to Eve,
As mother said in jest,
Uttered in dead earnest.

Bloodshed

And Lord one final thing:
May I never be caught in the
Firing line between two academics
In a tug-of-war with no heel—
Ropes hymning it to a higher
Source stymieing the ego
May I never become their accordion.

(Pause)

The Ethnographer

"How many kids do you have?
How many head of cattle?"
The ethnographer showers a
Deluge of queries on the native
Who invariably chips in a curt
Antiphony: "I am blessed."

*Tight-lipped stiff as though I
Am a cattle rustler or a baby snatcher albino
Can't understand the logic of the native
Secretive overprotective of mundane matters*

"How much money do you have
in your savings account?"

A question shot in the dark
Silence in the room
As the one directed at frowns
Purses her lips
Barely hiding her irritation with
A question so uncalled for
Gathers her temper smiles
In order not to lunge for my head

"What sort of dumb question is that?
Surely, it is none of your business."

One hears the sable rattle of the teeth

Can't understand the logic of the ethnographer
Secretive overprotective of matters mundane

What harm is done
In prying into her personal finances?

Buyer of yarns about foreign lands
Beware outlandish voices
Purveyors of pulp who refuse to remember
All monkeys see the uncovered
Rump of the monkey next door.

V

Where to, Africa?

Tell me.
Tell me what silence follows
the final silence
spun from the very fall of the sun?
What is it, Phoenix?
Give me a word,
a sign.

—Adonis, "Elegy in Exile"

Soporific Gestations

The left eye dozes off
While the right eye that has bred sleep
All its life now wards off
Soporific gestations kept at bay
By a sty shooting out
From the base of a peripheral blind spot
Keeping ajar the halls of remembrance
For a memory run out of town
During the first era of the Silent Trade
That dumped muscatel and sugar cubes
On innocent palates.

North African Blues

The season of the purveyors of
Farts forbidden in their backyard
Starts anew

Each year at its allotted time
The sirens herald the visitation of the
Locust laden with cash

The tourist guide—a broken record reamer
Replete with ancient glories long forgotten
Ancient glories no longer remembered—
Retraces the route in the ancient *kasbah*
Espying the footprints which took Tarik to
The Rock on the other side of the sea

There is a tinge of pride in his voice as he
Reels off a few dazzling stratagems of the old master
Stratagems that reverberate in the bus among a
Group of seasoned buyers dreaming of bargains
In the bazaar where native pride is sold to the highest
Bidder.

Labyrinths

In the leery weary labyrinths of an old emaciated hall
Lay stacked against a wall and in order of their inverse
Coating embroidered shell beads that signal
Transgressions wrought on the mettle of a
Giant mass unbeholden to itself

I go through the stacks not to bemoan a day
Against an old hag that bewitched suitors
From afar and across oceans
Not even to belabor the devious double dipping of
A homegrown lout that ran with the hare and
Denuded with the locust

I go through the quirky squeaky shelves
With the pace of one unable to tarry any longer
On the shores of what had been
Yet what has been—the suitor's early
Moments of razzle dazzle—and what is—
My dazed moments of never-ending stocktaking
Expeditions dilly-dally with inchoate moments
Of a resurrection foretold but difficult to
Divine.

Nocturnal Musings

Under a latticed moonlight lassoed from
Ages ago we spoke of communal odes
Of inaugurating the self in the smithy of the collective being
Of synchronizing seminal goals contiguous
With our euphoric primeval soul

The morning after
Defiant clouds perching too close to
Earth bullied the cleats anchoring the self
The rainspout on the left corner of my humble abode
Still eavesdropping on our nocturnal
Musings ruptured in ecstatic agony flooding
Thatched homes at the base of the valley

In panic every man ran to embrace his own
As delight cajoled my feet into dancing
The abhorred dance.

Petals of Manure
(With apologies to Ngugi wa Thiong'o)

Death is very much like life and
Life is the flip side of death
Yet what I saw in Africa was neither
Death nor life. Wraith-like wreaths
Hombres without objects
Objects without shadows
Tin drums tattooed with marks
Obscene like the footprints that strutted
Back and forth the place long before the locust

Perplexed by its mystic-like void
Foreseen only in some prophetic calamity
By she who was privy to that which was to come
By she who could steal a glimpse of the embryo in the
Bosom of the barren lot that was to inaugurate a
Succession of wild leaves unable to
Foster a new beginning

I become giddy with the violence that grazes
On human pasture as I run to parley with
The soul before milling into the crowd

Petals of manure still abound the horizon
Strands of life untapped still lurk in the
Bosom of the barren lot.

Crystal Balls

The lady sorcerer divines the future by reading the
Entrails of the only ram on the homestead. Strange intestines.
She refutes the findings of a male magician for faulty
Crystal balls. She divines. Flinches. Refocuses.
"Let me see the cup!" The cup is no better. Squints.
The view from her eyes belies the calm she attempts to exude.
She squints. Admonishes the rind that begot the incense
suffusing the Shrine. "How could this perfect cup produce
such a crooked view of the future? Which is in motion? The
corner? The unwholesome rind? Or me?" Still at the still
point. At last, someone reminds her of the source of the
entrails used for divination. She hollers, "From a pig's
stomach? How did the ram's entrails morpheme
into a pig's?"
Still at the still point. Still a stillborn.

(Pause)

Ali Jimale Ahmed

Which Is It?

How does it vomit fire and lava
Exhausting itself to death
Yet remain a volcano?

Is it a purging of the soul
Of undergoing a tantric ritual
Of expiating hubric grandeur to
Atone for illusions illumined
By the frailty of life under its feet
And down the slope?

Is it excess energy accrued in
A life of slumber? Or, a coming out
Of hibernation induced eons on end
By soporific incantations meant to buy
Time for those at the foot of the mountain?

VI

The Aloe Taste of Exile

Is the self ever to blame?
If not, then who?

—Nuruddin Farah,
Yesterday, Tomorrow:
Voices from the Somali Diaspora

Ali Jimale Ahmed

Strands in the Diaspora

Some are in Helsinki
Dawdling the day away
At the subway station in the center of town

Some are loitering at Stazione Termini
In Rome waiting for the latest news
From a home that no longer remembers them

Some are chewing their way out of angst
In rat-infested flats in London

Others are living out their final days
In tenements spread across state lines
In North America

The privileged are double dipping
As intellectual warlords bereft
Of all communicative ethics

Some are warmongering
Behind cloaks and with hidden
Daggers all intent on carving a piece
Of the now in the image of the old
Leftover nostalgia out of place
Out of sync with the here and now

The sane eerily joke about,
About finding their halcyon days
In far-flung places on Mother Earth
Where, altruism or no, someone
Is still willing to dole out
Parcels of recycled gifts
Reserved in their multiple names
Carved from a multiplicity of moieties
Still dancing to mangled tunes

Left behind by bones of dust
A few mad ones
Here and there
Stretch to embrace
Muffled tributaries unable to
Limp through a quicksand,
Quiescent quicksand mistaken for
The pre-dawn of happy days

The walking dead know
What wounds they bear

Ali Jimale Ahmed

Postmodern Coffins

In redolent multicolored coffins
The dead are buried in style
In Ghana

A pauper friend of yonder, I hear
Was left to wither in the streets
Of Accra: the first sunflower in our backyard
That defied a curfew imposed
By erstwhile septic men basking
In the glory of semi-perennial sunshine

In Accra, a pauper friend of yonder
Now rests in a Mercedes coffin
Six feet under
The clan's contributions
Got him his wish
In death when, for far less *cedis*[4]
He could have kicked the consumptive
Bout that led him to an early grave

Beside him lay the remains of a *trokosi*[5]
An odalisque interned in a boat-shaped
Cubicle paid for by a grieving husband-master.

[4] The Cedi is the Ghanaian currency.
[5] "Wife of the gods," or "a slave of a deity."

A Portrait of the Artist as a Ventriloquist
(for Nuruddin Farah)

"Women are from a crooked rib," he said
Shedding light on the inanities
Of naked needles unable to
Churn out sweet and sour milk—
The milkshake of the nomad

Cherche la mare
Cherche la femme to bake
Sardines for the famished
Cajole the women to conjure up
A sesame seed sprouting
In the bosom of a close sesame

If that didn't work, look elsewhere
The *dhebed*[6] bird pointed to
Maps that warped the mind
And if that, too, didn't work, the bird suggested
We forego old sayings and look
A gift horse in the mouth—
How long are you willing to
Fester in its stead

If maps and gifts couldn't help
Diagnose the malady of the corporeal
Perhaps the spirit is aching
Send a psychiatrist to the rescue
Through abreactions the secrets will be out
All that happened yesterday
And all that will happen tomorrow
Converge on the horizon
Eureka! The missing links are now found

---

[6] *Dhebed* (hoopoe): In Somali legend, this bird is said to be a harbinger of events yet to come.

All along you have been looking for yourself
Embark on a journey
Into the Netherlands of hell
Face the inferno of an elusive soul
Oh self, *Tunaenda wapi*?[7]
Stay tuned.

[7] *Tunaenda wapi* (Kiswahili): "Where are we going/Where we going?"

The Aloe Taste of Exile

Some are in J'burg, some in Adelaide
And the aloe taste of exile
Is like poisoned milk

After Anna Akhmatova